GREENLAND

in pictures

By BERNADINE BAILEY

VISUAL
GEOGRAPHY
SERIES

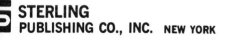
STERLING
PUBLISHING CO., INC. NEW YORK

Oak Tree Press Co., Ltd.
London & Sydney

VISUAL GEOGRAPHY SERIES

Afghanistan
Alaska
Argentina
Australia
Austria
Belgium and Luxembourg
Berlin—East and West
Brazil
Bulgaria
Canada
The Caribbean (English-
 Speaking Islands)
Ceylon
Chile
Colombia
Czechoslovakia
Denmark
Ecuador

Egypt
England
Ethiopia
Fiji
Finland
France
French Canada
Ghana
Greece
Greenland
Guatemala
Hawaii
Holland
Honduras
Hong Kong
Hungary
Iceland

India
Indonesia
Iran
Iraq
Ireland
Islands of the
 Mediterranean
Israel
Italy
Jamaica
Japan
Kenya
Korea
Kuwait
Lebanon
Liberia
Malawi

Malaysia and Singapore
Mexico
Morocco
Nepal
New Zealand
Norway
Pakistan
Panama and the Canal
 Zone
Peru
The Philippines
Poland
Portugal
Puerto Rico
Rumania
Russia
Saudi Arabia

Scotland
South Africa
Spain
Surinam
Sweden
Switzerland
Tahiti and the
 French Island
 the Pacific
Taiwan
Tanzania
Thailand
Tunisia
Turkey
Venezuela
Wales
West Germany
Yugoslavia

*The young people of Greenland enjoy table te
in their youth clubs.*

 The publishers wish to thank the following persons and organizations for photographs and illustrations use
this book: Danish Consulate General, New York; Danish Embassy, London; Danish Tourist Board, London; I
Danish Ministry of Foreign Affairs, Copenhagen; Scandinavian Airlines; Stella Reid; and the author, Bernadine B

'n good firm ground, a team of about 10 dogs can pull a sledge at a speed of 20 kilometres (about 12 miles) an hour. The Eskimo driver uses a long whip to urge the dogs on.

CONTENTS

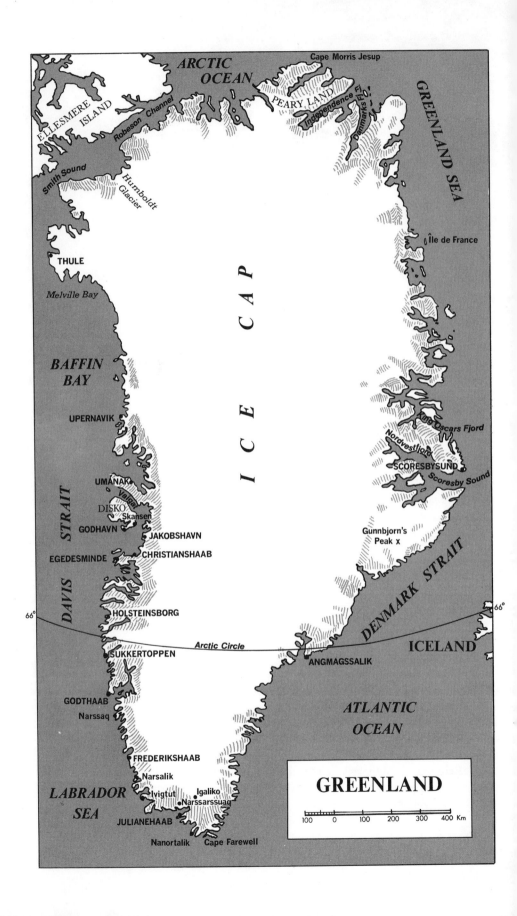

Most of the interior of Greenland is one big mass of ice, but ships can go up the fjords a short distance in the summer.

I. THE LAND

REENLAND IS the largest island in the world. has an area of 840,000 square miles, three mes the size of Texas and seven times the ze of the British Isles. It lies between the orth Atlantic Ocean and the Polar Sea, or rctic Ocean, separated from Canada's Arctic ands by Davis Strait and Baffin Bay, and om the Canadian mainland by the Labrador a. On the east the vast island fronts on the reenland Sea, an arm of the Arctic Ocean, and Denmark Strait, which separates it from eland, 250 miles away at the nearest point. uth of Denmark Strait, Greenland's eastern ores look out upon the Atlantic Ocean.

Its southern tip is about on a level with Britain's Shetland Islands or with Seward, Alaska, while its northern tip is only 6 degrees of latitude from the North Pole.

Cape Farewell, at the southern tip of Greenland, is 1,800 miles northeast of New York City. Canada and Greenland are separated in some places by 400 or more miles of icy water, but at the far northern tip they are less than 5 miles apart. A man could paddle this short distance if the sea were not frozen solid or filled with icebergs.

The shore line is cut up into hundreds of deep bays, with high rocky cliffs on either side.

One of the wonders of nature to be seen in Greenland—tons of snow and ice breaking off from a glacie and falling into Prince Christian's Sound.

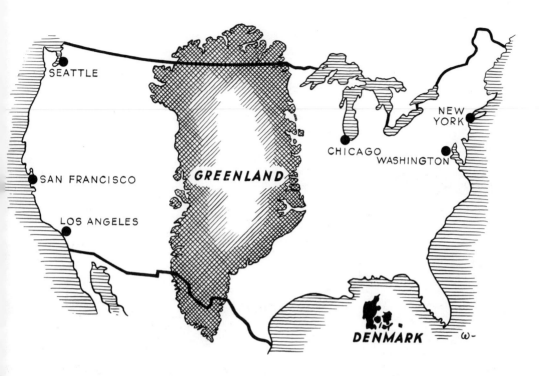

Greenland, if superimposed on the map of the United States, would flow over into Canada and Mexico. Note the small size of Denmark, included here for purposes of comparison.

fjords up to 186 miles long cut their way into the coast-line, which is about 24,500 miles long. In other words, the coast-line of this giant island is equal in length to the distance round the earth at the Equator! Many smaller islands lie close to Greenland's coast, the largest of which is Disko, where a number of hot springs exist. In the coastal areas, many small streams flow into the fjords.

ICE-CAP, GLACIERS AND ICEBERGS

There is no land quite like Greenland anywhere else in the world—not even Antarctica, which has no permanent population, and no large land animals.

Except for a narrow green band along the coast, Greenland is a mass of high mountains covered with a thick sheet of ice. From the air it looks like a plateau, because the valleys between the mountain peaks are filled with ice.

It is often impossible to tell where one mountain ends and another begins!

This plateau of ice lies between 6,000 and 10,000 feet above sea level. The ice averages about 1,000 feet in thickness, and in the deepest valleys it is 8,000 feet thick.

Gigantic glaciers slide down from the Greenland ice-cap, breaking up into majestic icebergs that float serenely down the still waters of the fjords, or inlets.

Glaciers force their way down every valley, and rocks and mountains of ice fall into the sea with a crash like a cannon. The Humboldt Glacier in northern Greenland is the largest in the Northern Hemisphere. Jakobshavn Glacier travels at the rate of a hundred feet a day and "calves" (sends an iceberg into the sea) on an average of every five minutes.

In summer, large icebergs float down the bays into the ocean. Most of the icebergs are bits of glacier that have broken off from the

After a huge piece of ice separates from a glacier, it breaks up into smaller pieces, which float down th[e] fjord toward the ocean.

huge ice sheet that covers most of Greenland all year long. Icebergs from Greenland's ice sheet have long endangered shipping in the North Atlantic. Icebergs are deceptive—only a small part of their mass shows above water, and many a ship has smashed into the huge submerged area and gone down.

The ice-cap is the last of the great ice sheets that once covered much of the Northern Hemisphere. When viewed from a plane on a sunny day, Greenland is a magnificent sight. The deep layer of ice reflects the sunshine and the landscape sparkles with the tints of the rainbow.

ICE-FLOES

Ice takes so many forms in all Greenland waters that there are more than a hundred terms in the Greenlandic language for the various ice phenomena. In addition to the icebergs from glaciers, massive ice-floes, sheets of ice formed in the Arctic Ocean and often more than 10 feet thick, drift south along the

When part of a glacier such as this one breaks o[ff] into the sea it can cause great destruction an[d] danger by creating huge waves, which often trav[el] 20 or 30 miles.

No one can live and nothing can grow in the interior of Greenland, which is a mass of ice, often several thousand feet thick.

...astern coast of Greenland, pass its southern ...ip, and move part way up the west coast.

Only 131,896 square miles of land along the ...oast, out of the total area, are free of ice. The ...mmense frozen area has a marked effect on the ...veather and climate of the entire Northern ...Iemisphere. It is often called the "weather ...actory" of the North Atlantic, and for this ...eason, is closely studied by meteorologists. If ...he Greenland ice-cap were to melt, the oceans ...f the world would rise by 25 feet!

MOUNTAINS

Greenland's highest mountains are found along the east coast, with many peaks of 7,000 feet or more. The highest mountain of all, Gunnbjorn's Peak, rises 12,500 feet above sea level. It is 62 miles from the coast, but on a clear, sunny day it may be seen from halfway out in Denmark Strait, between Iceland and Greenland. No doubt it was the first bit of land seen by the earliest Viking explorers, who

In this part of southern Greenland, there is no rim of green vegetation around the coast. Here the high, bare mountains plunge directly into the sea.

9

In this valley once covered by a glacier, which is now retreating a few inches a year, many low plants flower in summer.

called it "Hvitserk," meaning "White Shirt." It is the highest peak within the Arctic Circle. Many other mountains show only their summits above the surface of the ice sheet. The west coast is lined by lower mountains, up to 6,000 feet high.

Gunnbjorn's Peak was named after the Viking, Gunnbjorn Ulfsson, who was the first European to reach Greenland, when he was driven off course by a storm. Not until 1935, however, did anyone succeed in reaching the top of this peak. In that year it was scaled by a party that included Ebbe Munck, Lord Chamberlain to the Household of the Heir to the Danish Throne; Lawrence Wager, a professor of geology; and the British polar explorer, Augustine Courtauld.

In southwestern Greenland, children of all ages like to sit out in the sun, on the fast-growing grass, during the short summer season.

The sun never sets during the months of the Midnight Sun, in summer. This picture shows Narssaq Fjord, in southwestern Greenland, well lighted at midnight.

WEATHER

Since most of Greenland lies north of the Arctic Circle, one would expect the weather to be cold the year round, and it is. In the summer, the temperature along the coast averages about 50° F (10° C). On the southwest coast, there is almost no frost in summer and the days can be fairly warm. In the middle of the day it seems even warmer, for the sun's rays are direct and brilliantly hot. Even in summer, though, snow may fall at any time.

During the winter, the temperature along the coast is below freezing all the time. Usually it is about 0° F (−18° C) or below. On the whole, the weather is very uncertain, with sudden changes from bright sunshine to dense fog or heavy snowfalls and biting winds.

Because of its far northern latitude, Greenland sees the sun at midnight during the summer months and has polar night all 24 hours in the winter. At Disko Bay, for example, the period of darkness lasts from five to seven weeks. During this season the Northern Lights, or Aurora Borealis, appear on the northern horizon in the form of a constant arc

During the weeks of the Midnight Sun, one can go fishing all night.

months, when there is only darkness, the peopl[e] count the days until the sun will shine again On the day that it is due to appear again, the[y] have parties, usually a "sun lunch," and dres[s] in their best clothes as if welcoming a dis[-] tinguished guest, as in truth they are. Th[e] luncheon table is placed near a window so tha[t] the sunshine can come in as the most welcom[e] guest of all. Up until 1950, the people had onl[y] oil lamps for light, but now electric light ha[s] been introduced into all Greenland towns.

FLORA AND FAUNA

The summer heat and the moisture from th[e] melting snow and ice permit growing of a grea[t] variety of the higher plants, as well as mosses lichens, and algae. The latter thrive best i[n] Peary Land, which is the most northern part o[f] Greenland.

or as red, green, and yellow strips of flickering light.

Throughout Greenland, the people are very conscious of the forces of nature, especially the movements of the sun. During the long winter

Except in the southern districts, the groun[d] throughout Greenland is permanently frozen in some places as deep as 2,300 feet. In th[e] sheltered areas of the southwest, however

In southern Greenland especially, daisies and other flowers grow in great profusion. Although th[e] summer season is short, the sun shines round the clock, bringing fast growth to plants

Greenland is an angler's paradise, and many visitors come especially for that sport. The hillsides here are covered with scrubby trees—the closest thing to a forest in Greenland.

there are birch and alder thickets 15 feet tall, as well as mountain ash. Low scrubby bushes of the heath family, dwarf willows, saxifrages, alpine roses, grasses and Iceland poppies are found in the ice-free areas, and in marshy districts, sedges and horsetails are plentiful. Altogether there are more than 4,000 different plant species in Greenland. Even in Peary Land, the most northern land mass in the world, there are more than 100 species of Pteridophyta (fern-like plants).

An amazing variety of mammals and birds survive in this frozen northland. Notable among the mammals are polar bears, polar foxes, lemmings, ermines, walruses, narwhals, belugas, seals, whales, musk oxen, wild reindeer, and mountain hares.

Among the land birds are gerfalcons, ptarmigans, snowy owls, and white-tailed eagles, while the sea birds include the eider duck, auk, guillemot, gull and tern.

In the waters off Greenland there are over 100 species of fish, including cod and halibut. Sharks, shrimp and molluscs are abundant, and in the streams and ponds, trout and salmon are found.

NATURAL RESOURCES

Coal is mined in some areas, chiefly Disko Island, and peat is dug for fuel and building purposes in many districts. Greenland is the chief source of cryolite (used in producing aluminum) in the world and also has sizable

The hospital in Umanak has its own power station, central heating, and X-ray installations, as do most of the Greenland hospitals.

deposits of marble. The soil is very poor, little more than crumbled rock in many places, and permits only the most limited growing of garden vegetables here and there. Yet geologists tell us that in remote ages Greenland had a temperate climate and supported forests of walnuts, magnolias and laurels!

TOWNS AND VILLAGES

Despite the uncertain climate and the plateau of ice that fills most of this huge island, there are a number of small towns and villages all along the coast. In fact, there are 158 "occupied places," but not one of them can be called a city. Most of the larger settlements are on the west coast, which is a more protected area. The farthest north is THULE, where there is an American military base and atomic plant. There is another American military base at Sondre Stromfjord in the south.

A considerable distance south of Thule is UPERNAVIK. which stretches for half a mile along a rocky shore, where Arctic storms blow fiercely all the year round. It is even nearer the top of the world than is the North Cape in Norway. From May 7 to August 7, the sun shines continuously through the 24 hours of the day. In spite of being so near the North Pole, the little town is a lively place. Besides a large church, a store, a hospital, and a number of houses, there is a dance hall, where the people have lively parties.

Some distance south of Upernavik is UMANAK. The name Umanak means "heart mountain," and the mountain itself is very difficult to climb. On the lower hillsides in summer grow various polar flowers of many hues. In the village itself there are a few old peat houses and also the only stone church in Greenland. A children's sanitarium was built here in the 1960's.

South of Umanak is JAKOBSHAVN. This town dates from 1741, and it was here that Knud Rasmussen, the famous explorer, was born. The Greenlandic name of Jakobshavn—Llulissatk—means "icebergs." It is indeed well named, for the glacier that here breaks off into the sea is one of the largest in the world, pouring out more than 20,000,000 tons of ice into the fjord each day. When a huge iceberg breaks off it sets up undersea waves 25 to 30 miles away, which rise to six feet in the narrow port and cause great destruction. New port installations built in 1960 have solved the problems created by these huge icebergs.

Directly west of Jakobshavn, on the coast of the island of Disko, is one of Greenland's two capitals, GODHAVN, founded in 1773. Because of the difficulties of transportation before the age of aircraft, it was necessary to have a capital (Godhavn) in the northern area and

At Jakobshavn, the silhouette of the church looks out upon a "church" of ice, complete with spire. Originally the town was called Llulissatk by the Greenlanders, a name which means icebergs. No town could have been more appropriately named.

Considerable ingenuity is used by the architects in planning housing to be built on such rocky terrain as that of Christianshaab.

another (Godthaab) in the southern area. Today, Godthaab has taken over most of the governmental functions.

CHRISTIANSHAAB, a short distance south of Jakobshavn, is a typical Greenlandic town. The shrimp factory, which is one of the most modern in the world, is the pride of the community. Christianshaab also boasts a very modern housing development, constructed between 1964 and 1968. The buildings of this development surround a large rock and are staggered to fit the contours of the terrain. The town also has a modern school, hospital, office block, and shops.

A modern apartment house on the mountainside above Holsteinborg is in striking contrast to the traditional wooden house next to it.

In the west, Holsteinborg, second largest town in Greenland, is the scene of much activity in summer.

EGEDESMINDE, south of Godhavn, is one of the three largest towns in Greenland. It was founded in 1759. A new student hostel has been built on concrete foundations adapted to the broken, rugged, rocky terrain, and designed so as to allow the water from melting ice to flow under it.

HOLSTEINSBORG, Greenland's second largest town, is situated on the west coast just north of the Arctic Circle. In Greenland, the Arctic Circle is often called the "dog frontier," because the famous Greenlandic sledge dog is not found south of this Circle. Holsteinsborg contains both older and modern types of

In winter, Holsteinborg looks very different. The fishing boats are all frozen in the port.

In the summer there is feverish building activity, as pictured here in Sukkertoppen.

buildings, and Greenland's only high school is located there. There is a large shipyard in Holsteinsborg, and a supermarket.

South of Holsteinsborg is SUKKERTOPPEN, where the mountains form a backdrop to the street scene. Here, too, are modern apartment buildings, and more such structures, eight to ten storeys high, are being planned and built. The town clusters around a complex of mountain crests, narrow valleys, and large and small islands, all of which give this town its special character. All building activities must of course take place in the summer.

GODTHAAB, in the south, is the largest

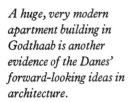

A huge, very modern apartment building in Godthaab is another evidence of the Danes' forward-looking ideas in architecture.

Godthaab, one of the two settlements originally established by the Vikings, is now a thriving modern town. It is expected to have a population of 15,000 by the year 1975.

town in Greenland and also its southern capital. It has the largest block of flats in the country, with 120 apartments, each with a small balcony and with modern installations.

Godthaab, whose name means Good Hope, dates from the year 1728, so it is one of the oldest towns in Greenland. Its situation was chosen with great care, so that it would be suitable for a mission, a trading post, and a military outpost. Also, the location made it

In Godthaab, the largest town in Greenland, a well stocked store supplies merchandise from Denmark and the United States.

Trout are popular game fish caught in the Kringua River, at the bottom of Narssarssuaq Fjord. Char, with its bright red belly, is the variety of trout most common in Greenland.

possible for the Governor to spot any unwelcome ships that might enter the nearby fjords.

When Godthaab was first settled by Europeans, about 200 Greenlandic families were living on the shores of the fjord. In 1733, the plague killed about 170 of them, but the colony continued to grow, and by 1760, it had a population of nearly 1,000. A wooden church was erected in 1758, and in 1849 the present church was built.

Today Godthaab is a modern town, with about 8,000 people, a modern college, hospital, shops, and homes, as well as government buildings.

Moravian missionaries came to Greenland in 1731 and settled in a large valley a little south of Godthaab. They called the place Ny Herrnhut (New Moravia). When the Moravian missionaries left Greenland in 1900, Ny Herrnhut was incorporated into the town of Godthaab.

In the far south is NARSSARSSUAQ, on the shore of Eric's Fjord. Here a landing field built during World War II, is now the headquarters of air communications for South Greenland. The United States established here a military base, Blue West I, in 1941, from which aircraft escorted the convoys on their way to Europe. When the Americans gave up the base in 1958, it was taken over by the Danish Ministry for Greenland.

Across the fjord are the ruins of the dwellings of Eric the Red and Leif Ericsson, discoverer of North America. Here also are the remains of the oldest church in the Western Hemisphere.

Narssarssuaq is surrounded by the sea and high mountains, and so no motor roads lead from it. The area has many historical associations, however, for it was at Eric's Fjord that the main Viking settlement was established. This settlement fell into decay by the end of the 12th century and was not explored again for 500 years. It was along the shores of Eric's Fjord that poems were composed about Attila, King of the Huns, and Siegfried, the Dragon-Slayer.

Farther south on Eric's Fjord is NARSSAQ, which with a population of a little over 1,000, is the second largest village in south Greenland. In 1880, the Royal Greenland Trading Company established a base here for seal hunting. In recent years, a fish factory has been built, a slaughterhouse, a shrimp cannery, and a factory for processing cod-liver oil. Today, Narssaq is a modern village with electricity and an ample water supply the year round, although water supplies often present quite a problem in Greenland. There are a cinema, a fire brigade, two schools, a restaurant, a printing works, and one of the best stores in Greenland.

Not far from Narssaq is the tiny village of IGALIKO, where the early Viking settlers had their open-air Parliament (called "Thing") and the Bishop had his headquarters. A Norwegian started farming here in 1790, and Igaliko is now the hub of a thriving agricultural area.

The remains of the ancient cathedral, built at Igaliko of sandstone in the 12th century, cover a large area. Leaders of the Church resided

Narssaq, in southwestern Greenland, has several fish canneries, most of which are located near the water to make it easier to ship the processed fish.

Into this fjord, now called Eric's Fjord, Eric the Red led 35 ships from Iceland, filled with families who settled in Greenland in A.D. 985.

Thanks to the efforts of the Royal Greenland Trade Department, there are modern stores in all Greenland towns. This one is in Jacobshavn.

here during the years 1124–1378, and from here expeditions went westwards to Labrador and Newfoundland and northwards to the walrus-hunting grounds. The skulls of walruses and narwhals have been found under the choir of the church, no doubt buried there in a superstitious belief that these animals would be easier to hunt if their bones were buried beside those of the chieftains in the cathedral itself. The cathedral was dedicated to St. Nicholas, patron saint of seafarers.

The principal settlement in east Greenland is ANGMAGSSALIK. A Danish expedition led by Gustav Holm came here in 1884 and found 416 Eskimos living like primitive people of the Stone Age. They were the last of the tribe that had once inhabited the east coast all the way from Peary Land in the north to Cape Farewell in the south. In 1894, the Royal Greenland Trading Company set up its first post in Angmagssalik. Then, 352 people were living there, while today 2,500 inhabitants of the Angmagssalik district are dependent for their living on fishing and seal hunting.

The well-known husky dog was brought to Greenland by the early Eskimo settlers.

2. HISTORY

IN SPITE of its bleak, Arctic nature, Greenland has been the goal of various migrations, since long before the days of the Roman Empire. Each of these waves of people left behind traces of their culture, which is how we know about them today. About 4,000 years ago, the first inhabitants of Greenland arrived there from Canada's Ellesmere Island by crossing over Smith Sound. They were primitive Stone-Age people who lived largely by hunting reindeer.

About a thousand years later, another group of people advanced along the eastern coast, while other tribes moved down the west coast. Archeologists call them the Sarkak. These people used cooking stones, which they heated and put in water. For light, they used small, circular blubber lamps of soapstone or sandstone. The dog was domesticated, but was not used as a beast of burden. They hunted seals

and fish with harpoons, and reindeer with bow-and-arrow. The climate at that time was mild, but about 500 B.C. it began to turn very cold. Because of the severe climate during the Iron Age, the coast of Greenland was deserted.

THE DORSET AND THULE PEOPLES

At about the beginning of the Christian Era, a new people arrived in Greenland, the so-called Dorset race. They left pictures of themselves in small carvings of wood and walrus ivory, and are mentioned in the oldest Greenland legends. They were strong men and great hunters of seal and walrus, but they had neither dogs nor kayaks. Bows and arrows were also unknown to them. They chased reindeer and then killed them with lances. The Dorset people are

The kayak was invented by the whale-hunting Thule people of the north. In winter, the kayak is placed high on a scaffolding so that the dogs cannot reach it and tear its seal-skin covering to pieces.

ERIC THE RED

In about the year 875, some Vikings (or Norsemen) from Iceland were blown off course by a storm and reported seeing the southern coast of Greenland. When Eric the Red, the son of a chieftain, was sentenced to three years' exile from Iceland in 981, he decided to go to this land in the west. At the end of the three years he returned to Iceland and began a promotion campaign that has probably never been surpassed. By calling the land Greenland —which connoted a picture of a productive, fertile area—he at once aroused the interest of the Icelanders. In the summer of 985, 35 vessels carrying a thousand men, women, and children set sail for the southern part of Greenland, an uninhabited area. Only 14 of the ships arrived, landing in a fjord which they named Eric's Fjord, in what is now the district of Julianehaab. These Icelanders were extremely tough peasant and hunting people, who soon took over the new land, and Eric became a great chief.

thought to be the first builders of igloos or snow huts.

In about the 12th century, a vigorous and pugnacious race of whale hunters, called the Thule people, spread over the Arctic. Perhaps the Dorsets were overcome by people of this more highly developed culture, which owed its superiority in part to the invention of the kayak and the umiak. The Thule people had large blubber lamps which not only lighted and heated their homes but also served as a stove for cooking. This was a great improvement over the small blubber lamp of the Dorset people, which was used only for lighting.

The relationship between these earlier people and the present population of Greenland is not clear. The Dorset and Thule people were undoubtedly of the same stock as the present Eskimos.

From Greenland, Leif Ericsson visited Markland (Labrador) nearly 1,000 years ago. He found the land flat and covered with forest, with extensive white sands, as shown in this picture of Cape Porcupine and The Strand.

Much information about Viking Greenland has been obtained from early runic stones. The runic alphabet used by the early Scandinavians was derived from the Roman.

LEIF ERICSSON

As was the custom of Viking chieftains, Eric the Red sent his son Leif to the court in Norway. Leif returned in the year 1000, bringing priests to preach Christianity in Greenland. Leif also brought the big news that he had been driven off course to the west, by a storm, and had there discovered a new land, which he called Vinland (Newfoundland). After this he was called Leif the Lucky.

A few attempts were made to colonize Vinland, but they came to nothing, because of the hostility of the natives whom they encountered. The Norsemen did bring back timber from this new land, which was badly needed in Greenland.

THE VIKINGS (NORSEMEN)

The Vikings established two settlements in Greenland—Julianehaab on the east coast and Godthaab on the west. For 500 years, these Vikings from Iceland lived by the deep fjords of southern Greenland. They built churches and monasteries, and the population grew to 4,000. They went on adventurous hunting expeditions in the far north, then sailed to Europe to sell walrus tusks, furs, seal-skins, and falcons. These regular sailings over the North Atlantic took place 500 years before the voyage of Columbus. The last account of such a voyage dates from 1347.

The Vikings stayed in Greenland until a change of climate and interrupted connections with Europe wiped out the settlements. Another reason why they perished was the appearance of the Eskimo hunters, who had come from the northwest. These people were hardened to the severe climate and had developed a hunting culture that was among the best in the world. They took over Greenland and in time the Europeans were all gone. It is not known, however, whether there was any actual conflict between the two races.

CHRISTIANITY

The Christian religion had no appeal for Eric the Red, but his wife, Thorhilde, soon became baptized. At a short distance from their farm, Thorhilde had a church built, the first in the New World. The people paid their tithes, or church taxes, in the form of walrus tusks. In time there were 17 parish churches and two monasteries in Greenland, and a bishopric was established at Igaliko in 1124. Literature was studied and sagas were written, as in Iceland. At least one of the famous Eddas, or books of Norse poetry, was composed in Greenland.

The ruins of Hvalsey Church, built in the 12th century, are still standing near Julianehaab.

Well preserved skeletons, and goods deposited with the dead, have been excavated near some of the medieval church ruins in Greenland. The clothing found in these graves was of the style of the 14th and 15th centuries.

In 1261, the Norsemen of Greenland agreed to pay a tax to the Norwegian king who, in return, sent a ship to Greenland every year with needed supplies. When the plague raged in Norway in 1349, communication with Greenland was cut off and the settlement of Godthaab had to be abandoned. In 1378, the last bishop of Igaliko died, and at about this time the Eskimos began to settle near Julianehaab.

On September 16, 1408, there was a wedding in Hvalsey Church. The newly married couple, who were both Icelanders, left Greenland two years later. From that point on, the history of Greenland vanishes in a mist of legend and guesswork, and there is no further evidence of Christianity in Greenland until 1721.

The walls of Hvalsey Church are still standing, and in the churchyard, articles of clothing have been found which are in the European fashions of the 15th century. What happened to the people themselves has remained an unsolved mystery.

THE YEARS OF OBLIVION, 1410-1721

For three centuries there was apparently no government in Greenland, and the Eskimos were supreme. Within the limits of the Greenlandic Stone Age, they created their own culture. They hunted the Greenland whale,

The ruins of a 15th-century Norse farm show the layout of the various rooms and buildings.

Archeological investigations in Greenland have revealed the ruins of 10 old churches and many relics, including this wooden cross, which dates from about A.D. 1001.

one of the largest creatures in the world, in boats made of skins.

In 1542, a caravel from the German city-state of Hamburg made its way to east Greenland but found no inhabitants. In 1548, the English navigator, Martin Frobisher, reached land on the west coast, not knowing that it was Greenland. In 1585, the English explorer, John Davis, found Eskimos in southwest Greenland and in the north around Upernavik. In 1607, a Danish expedition searched the west coast for Norsemen, but without success.

In 1612, the English sent an expedition to Greenland, but the Greenlanders killed its leader, James Hall, after sentencing him for kidnapping. During the 17th century, Dutch, English, Basque, Norwegian, and Danish whalers sailed into Greenland waters in order to obtain whale oil for lighting and whalebone for combs, umbrella ribs, etc. As many as 1,000 whales were killed in a season.

The growing interest in Greenland on the part of the English and Dutch, as well as the profitable expeditions of the first whalers, whetted the appetite of King Christian IV of Denmark. He sent four expeditions to Greenland in the years 1605, 1606, and 1607, and

then declared the country to be the property of the Danish Crown. The expeditions tried to find earlier Norsemen and also searched for minerals, but were not successful in either mission. The Danes did bring back five Eskimos, who created a sensation in Europe. More Eskimos were carried off in 1652, to be presented to King Frederik III at Gottorp Palace, and they soon after died of measles.

SEARCH FOR THE NORTHWEST PASSAGE

For several centuries, explorers (and their monarchs) were obsessed with the idea of finding a shorter sea route from Europe to the riches of the Orient than around South Africa. In 1476, King Christian I of Denmark fitted out the first expedition which attempted to reach China and India by way of Greenland. They were not able to land in Greenland, but they scratched a compass on a rock face to show that they had taken possession of the land.

In 1621, Christian IV sent Jens Munks with two warships, but he was forced to find winter quarters in Hudson's Bay. His journal describes nine years of hardship, during which 52 men died. The many unsuccessful attempts to find a northwest passage to India led in time to the rediscovery of Greenland.

It is no wonder that when first taken to Europe, the Eskimos created a sensation. Their native costumes are both beautiful and practical.

After Eric the Red, Hans Egede, whose statue stands here, probably played a bigger rôle in the development of Greenland than any other one person.

HANS EGEDE

The real colonizer of Greenland was a Norwegian clergyman, Hans Egede (1686–1758), who had developed an interest in the country through reading and also through personal contacts in his youth. He interested the merchants of Bergen, Norway, in the idea of establishing a Greenland trading company in 1719. Two years later he landed in Greenland with three ships and re-established the colony of Godthaab. To his great disappointment, he found none of the old Norsemen, only utterly strange Eskimo people.

With the help of his courageous wife, Gertrud Rask, Hans Egede embarked on a work that began a new chapter in Greenland history. The Vikings of the first settlement of Greenland were Roman Catholics. In the Reformation, however, all of Scandinavia adopted the Lutheran form of Protestantism. Egede opened a Lutheran mission station in Godthaab in 1728. The first Danish trading post was also established in that year.

When the new king, Christian VI, ordered that the mission be discontinued and that all its members return, in 1731, Egede stayed behind. For 15 years he continued to preach the gospel

to the Greenlanders. He was beloved by the entire population and called the Apostle of Greenland.

In 1733, the King sent out three missionaries of the Moravian Church, a sect that originated in what is now Czechoslovakia. Their ship brought the bubonic plague, which spread through the district and killed most of the people. When Egede's wife died of the disease, he left Greenland, but directed the Greenland mission from Copenhagen until his death in 1758.

With the return of Christianity, books also reappeared in Greenland, but religion and literature both had a hard struggle to spread along the winding coast of this huge island. Missionary work continued into the 20th century—the last pagans were baptized in 1922.

EXPLORATION AND TRADE

About 1820, William Scoresby of England navigated the great complex of fjords on the east coast, and in 1823, a fellow Englishman named Clavering discovered an island off the northeast coast, where he encountered many

Eskimos. In 1883–84, Gustav Holm and T. V. Garde, both Danes, spent the winter in Greenland and definitely established that there were no Viking survivors in east Greenland. They found a small Eskimo tribe, which was declining because of poor hunting and feuding.

A few years later, the famous Norwegian explorer, Fridtjof Nansen, together with some Lapp skiers, penetrated deep into the ice-cap south of Disko Bay. Nansen was the first to use skis in exploring Greenland, and he also devised a new and lighter type of sledge, which could be hauled without dogs. He invented the Nansen cooker, which made it possible to cook two hot meals a day on a week's supply of one quart of oil. On August 22, 1888, Nansen and five companions set out on skis from Angmagssalik. They reached Godthaab Fjord, a distance of 375 miles, in 42 days.

Knud Rasmussen, who was born and grew up in Jakobshavn, spent the winter of 1903–04 with Eskimos in the Cape York district. Beginning in 1912, he led the Thule expeditions, which gathered information about polar geography as well as Eskimo life and customs. On the fifth Thule expedition, Rasmussen and two others made the longest sledge journey in history—6,000 miles across Arctic North America. On this trip they re-established broken links between Eskimo tribes in Greenland and those in Alaska. This was the last of the old-time sledge expeditions in Greenland. From this time on, all exploring and development were done by scientists, working in large groups and aided by every modern technical device: aircraft, wireless, radar, electric power, and so on.

The trading post set up in 1728 had gradually gained a firm footing, and, by 1759, a chain of trading stations had been established from Frederikshaab to Umanak. When the Danish government found that the Greenlanders were often exploited by the traders it took over all trade and established the Royal Greenland Trade Department. This monopoly was main-

This memorial was erected to Knud Rasmussen in the town where he was born, Jakobshavn.

tained down to 1950 and was of the greatest importance in protecting the Greenland community and its development.

For more than 150 years, the prime object of Denmark's policy in Greenland was to shelter the special way of life of the island's hunting community from harmful outside influences. The need for outside connections was not very great. When sealing began to decline and it became clear that fishing would have to take its place, it seemed necessary to change the policy regarding Greenland. The fish had to be processed and exported, and therefore outside connections became necessary.

DENMARK'S SOVEREIGNTY

Denmark's sovereignty over Greenland was first internationally recognized by an exchange of notes with the Russian government in 1782. It was a long time, however, before Danish sovereignty over the unoccupied areas of Greenland gained general recognition. In 1924, the Norwegians refused to recognize Danish control of unoccupied east Greenland. The dispute came before the International Court of Justice at The Hague, which gave a decision for Denmark in 1933.

When the Germans occupied Denmark in 1940, the government's representatives in Greenland applied to the United States for assistance in regard to defence and supplies. The following year, the United States recognized Denmark's sovereignty over Greenland, and at the same time arranged for American military bases at Narssarssuaq and Sondre Stronfjord, with an air base and atomic plant at Thule.

After World War II, a commission made up of Danish and Greenlandic politicians was instructed to form a new policy for Greenland. On the basis of their report, a radical change in the island's social and economic structure was introduced. The former trade monopoly was abolished and Greenland was opened up to development by outside capital and initiative.

In 1953, Greenland was made a part of Denmark by an amendment to the Constitution, and Greenlanders assumed the same rights and obligations as the inhabitants of Denmark.

The Greenlanders had fought one of the hardest struggles in history against the pitiless forces of nature and against exploitation by outsiders. Today, the communities of Greenland are no longer struggling in primitive isolation—they are fast becoming modernized and building up a prosperous economy. It is truly an amazing accomplishment in a polar land with so few natural resources.

Like most Greenlanders, these children, playing in the summer sunshine of southern Greenland, are of mixed Eskimo and Scandinavian extraction.

This schoolboy shows clearly his mixed Eskimo and Scandinavian lineage.

3. THE PEOPLE

WHEN THE Danish colonization of Greenland began, the Danes found a distinctive and widely developed Eskimo culture. It was so strange to them that they did not even consider it a culture. Nevertheless, the Eskimos at first were able to assert themselves over the newcomers on their own terms. Eventually, however, they had to yield, and many of them retreated to remote localities. In time, most of them lost their distinctive creative ability, and the legends that had been handed down for centuries were replaced by Danish folk tales.

Hymn singing replaced the spontaneous music of the Eskimos, and Eskimo poetry also went into oblivion. Except for a small group in the Thule area, the Greenlanders of today are a mixture of Eskimo and Danish blood.

The Eskimos had always been a very self-reliant people. They invented the kayak by covering a framework of bone or wood with de-haired seal-skin. This light craft enabled them to hunt marine animals in the sea itself, especially seals and whales. They learned to attack the animals with harpoons fixed to a long

The kayak is still used for hunting. An air bladder (the oval, white object at the right) helps to keep the seal afloat as the hunter starts toward home.

line kept afloat by an air-filled bladder. This arrangement prevents even the largest animals from being lost below the water. The umiak, a larger, open craft made in the same way as the kayak, was used for fishing and transporting families and possessions. For use on the ice, the Eskimos built a sledge, drawn by strong and persevering Greenland dogs.

The talents and artistic expressions of the Eskimos were not lost, however. They were merely subdued for a time. In the 1850's, a Danish official, H. J. Rink, realized that these people needed to regain their self-respect and self-reliance. He encouraged them to write their old legends and he had them published

Children today play on the same type of sledge devised by their Eskimo ancestors long ago.

People of Thule gather in front of the local school. All the inhabited areas of Greenland have schools and churches.

in Greenlandic and Danish. He also began a monthly magazine in Greenlandic, in order to encourage Greenlandic literature.

THE POLAR ESKIMOS OF THULE

The narrow coastal strip called Thule, which lies in the northwest of Greenland, is about the size of Denmark. The steep coastal cliffs are broken by glaciers, and the sea is frozen for most of the year. The long winter night lasts for four months and the period of the midnight sun is also four months long. The temperature ranges from —58°F (—16° C) to 43°F (6° C).

In this bleak area, the Eskimo people have proven themselves to be intelligent and capable, as well as considerate and helpful and have preserved their ancient culture and racial purity. The great Danish and American Arctic expeditions, carried out with dog sledges, would

not have been possible without the co-operation of these remarkable people. Travellers and explorers in the Arctic are always made welcome by them and given a hearty meal of boiled seal, walrus or polar bear. The Eskimos look after those of their own people who are old or sick or unable to hunt. Best of all, they are always cheerful and smiling.

From such animals as the bear, seal, and walrus, they obtain all their requirements—

Many families in Greenland still live by catching seals. The man on the left is putting his knife in the carcass to start the process called flensing— that is, removing the hide and cutting up the blubber.

This mother and baby from Thule, in the far north, are well protected with their sealskin coat and hood.

clothes from the animal skins, lighting and heating from the blubber, and nourishing food from the flesh. All their other requirements they make themselves, including their dwellings. In winter, their houses are made of stones and turf, and in summer they are lightly constructed skin tens that can be carried about on their migrations. The people of Thule are the only Eskimos of Greenland who still build the igloo, or snow hut. However, they only use it as a temporary shelter on hunting forays. Through the long lonely winters they amuse themselves by carving in ivory (from walrus tusks) and reciting poems and stories that have come down through the centuries.

1756373

The Greenlanders are a smiling, happy race. These women are wearing ornaments made of bone and ivory.

35

Many Greenlanders have considerable craft and artistic abilities, which they express in their clever carvings, as this man is doing.

The Greenlanders' carvings in bone or ivory often show striking originality.

These figures, called "tupilaks," are usually carved from the teeth of sperm whales.

36

This present-day wooden carving by a Green-lander shows typically Eskimo features.

A NEW WAY OF LIFE

When hunting was the principal occupation, most Greenlanders lived in small, scattered settlements, so that each group could have its own wide range in which to hunt. When fishing became the main occupation, the people found it an advantage to concentrate in townships. Fish have to be cut up and frozen, and it is more efficient to do this in a few large factories than in many small installations. It is also easier and cheaper to supply a population with food, education, medical care, and other services when they live in townships than when they are scattered over a wide area.

This change took place after World War II, when the government encouraged the people to move to such "open water" (ice-free) sites as Godthaab, Holsteinsborg, Sukkertoppen, and Frederikshaab. In these four communities there is the possibility of developing all-season fishing.

In the hunting districts of the northwest and the east coast, the population remains scattered. In the extreme south, where there is sheep-breeding, flocks must be moved into new areas, from time to time, in order to find grazing land.

GROWTH IN POPULATION

In 1950, the population of Greenland was about 23,000, but it has been growing rapidly, especially for an area where living is so difficult. By 1973, the population had doubled, and there were 48,000 people living on the island. Of this total, 17 per cent, or about 7,000, were born in Denmark. The population is expected to reach 65,000 by the year 1985.

Wearing one's hair in a topknot is a style popular with older Eskimos.

37

The Greenlanders have had to accustom themselves to many new ways, including self-service stores where they buy most of their necessities.

who held the top positions, received higher wages, and had more material benefits. The Greenlanders recognized that equality could come only through education and a knowledge of the Danish language. Demands for educational reforms and the teaching of Danish were out forward. Danish teachers were sent to Greenland and their influence became so strong that the Greenlandic language was partly supplanted. Feeling between the two races still exists, but is gradually being worked out as the economy expands and education becomes more general.

DANES VS. GREENLANDERS

The Danes came to Greenland with superior education and a higher standard of living than the Greenlanders. It was only natural that friction should arise between the two. The Eskimos resented the domination of the Danes,

LANGUAGE

The Eskimo dialects of Greenland, Canada, Alaska and a tiny stretch of Siberia are not known to be related to any other language group. Totally distinct from the American Indian tongues, they show some resemblance to Chukchi, which is spoken in a small corner of eastern Siberia.

The Greenlandic language is derived from an Eskimo dialect with the addition of some Danish words. Written in the Latin alphabet,

Girls of Julianehaab enjoy their lessons in cooking, given by a Danish teacher.

This school at Sukkertoppen shows the new trend toward larger units, in contrast to the small isolated buildings of the past.

it is the only Eskimo tongue to possess a written literature and an official status.

Greenlandic is extremely complex, differing greatly from Danish and English in its structure. It is extremely difficult for a European to master—yet its phonetic system is simple, and a Dane can pronounce it readily even if he cannot communicate in it.

A lively language debate has been taking place in Greenland in recent years, especially among the young people who are eagerly searching for a new identity. The schools are dominated by teachers from Denmark, because there are not enough Greenlandic and bilingual teachers. This means that when children first go to school, they must learn a new language. Often they must learn Danish from teachers who cannot speak Greenlandic. The Greenlanders are quite willing to learn Danish, but not at the expense of doing away completely with their own language. The Danish officials realize the importance of this problem. They also know that Greenlanders need to recover their self-respect and inner security. It seems that the means of accomplishing these goals will be through a knowledge of the Danish language.

EDUCATION

Since half the population is under 15 years of age and all education is free, the educational system causes a heavy tax burden. There are 100 schools, but 34 of them have fewer than 20 children each, while others have as many as 1,000. Attached to most of the larger schools are hostels, where children from remote areas can live and have their meals. Youngsters attend school in Greenland up to the age of 15, and a little over 1,000 children are

Children in school pay close attention, for they are eager to learn.

sent each year to schools in Denmark for higher education. Through scholarships and state loans, any Greenlander may obtain the education he wants and for which he is qualified.

Craftsmen, navigators, machine operators, shop and office workers are trained at the central technical school at Godthaab. A growing number of Greenlanders who go to Denmark for education decide to stay there. About 4,000 are now living in Denmark, many of them married to Danes who have worked in Greenland.

THREE KINDS OF COMMUNITIES

The 158 occupied places in Greenland fall into three categories—township, settlement, and outpost. The largest community is called a *township*, of which there are 19. They are not really towns, because even those with the largest population would not fill a single block of a modern city. Jakobshavn, with about 2,000 people, is a typical medium-sized township. The local government council consists of nine members, including four from outlying settlements.

Jacobshavn is one of the oldest settlements in Greenland, founded in 1741. Now it has about 1,850 inhabitants, three of whom are seen here.

Kallico is a typical Greenland settlement, not large enough to be called a town. A medieval church once stood near the water—now only the ruins remain.

Akunak, not far from Egedesminde, is typical of the 121 *settlements*. With a population of about 220, Akunak is represented by one member of the municipal board of Egedesminde. In this settlement, there is a Trading Company shop, a postal depot, and a municipal workshop. A teacher trained at a Danish college and a Greenlander teach 42 children in two classes at the local school. A public bath, with hot water, has been set up in connection with the school.

Cape Hope, in the Scoresbysund area on the east coast, is an *outpost*, with about 125 inhabitants, who still live mostly by hunting. The local school chapel is used for church services and for teaching, and with the help of private contributions, an assembly building has been erected.

Besides townships, settlements, and outposts, there are 18 radio and weather stations, which actually have very little to do with Greenland itself. Located on the east coast, they are manned by Danes, and provide information for shipping and air transport in the North Atlantic.

Godthaab, in southern Greenland, is not only the largest town, but is also the seat of government.

4. GOVERNMENT

SINCE 1774, the Danish government has taken care of many responsibilities toward the population of Arctic Greenland. In the eternal struggle against a savage climate and violent forces of nature, the Royal Greenland Trade Department was like a safety net which enabled the country to develop. For 200 years, the men in this organization have, by their pioneering efforts, laid the foundation for the Greenland people's material and cultural progress. Under the most adverse conditions, they have kept the land supplied with essential goods. They have developed means of communication to secure the long supply lines between Greenland and Denmark.

After Greenland officially became the property of the Danish Crown, the Danish flag (white cross on red ground) was prominently displayed.

THE MINISTRY OF GREENLAND

In Denmark, the Ministry of Greenland handles the affairs of the island, with the help of various departments. The Greenland Technical Organization takes charge of technological development and planning. The Royal Greenland Trade Department keeps Greenland supplied with all necessaries at uniform prices everywhere, and it also has charge of all exports of Greenland products. The Greenland Geological Survey is responsible for geological exploration, and it controls data for oil companies, mining companies, and the like.

The Minister for Greenland is also Minister for Fisheries. He is assisted by a consultative council of Greenlandic and Danish politicians in Copenhagen. All important posts in his department are filled by officials who have served in the province, and he himself travels frequently to Greenland. This huge island is so different, in many ways, from other Danish provinces that a special ministry is necessary.

Certain matters relating to Greenland, however, have been transferred to other departments. In 1965, for example, the police were placed under the Ministry of Justice. Also, broadcasting now comes under the Ministry for Cultural Affairs. The Ministry for Greenland, however, will probably be necessary for many years, because of the need for co-ordinating local and specialized knowledge. So far, no Greenland politician has expressed a desire for anything but the closest connection between Denmark and Greenland.

The Greenland Council is an independent body of advisors to the Minister for Greenland. Of the Council's eleven members, one is appointed by the Crown, three are elected by the Greenland Provincial Council, two are Greenland members of the Folketing (Parliament), and the remaining five are members of the Folketing who are nominated by the five major political parties.

DANISH POLICY

Since the middle of the 19th century, Danish policy has been designed to protect the native population of Greenland and to help it attain greater responsibility for its own affairs. In the Danish Parliament, the members from Greenland speak as freely as the other elected representatives.

While many countries have broken away from their colonial rulers, in Greenland there has so far been no conflict or movement to break away, yet some Danes and Greenlanders feel that Greenlandic independence will come eventually. The status of Greenland is the wish of its people, as expressed through their elected representatives. A desire for closer co-operation with Denmark has been emphasized on various occasions. This attitude was shown especially when King Frederik and Queen Ingrid of Denmark visited Greenland in 1968.

Since 1950, the annual Danish Government expenditure in Greenland has increased 15-fold. Half of this goes to new investment and the

A meeting of the Greenland Provincial Council is in progress.

other half to the running of public institutions, of which education and health have taken the largest share.

THE GREENLAND PROVINCIAL COUNCIL

The highest elected body in Greenland itself is the Provincial Council, which is so constituted as to enable every Greenland view and opinion to find expression. Made up of 16 to 21 members elected for four-year terms, this Council drafts local regulations and levies taxes on certain goods. No law affecting Greenland is passed by the Danish Parliament until the Provincial Council of Greenland has been consulted, and no legislation is passed against the wishes of the Greenlanders. Local self-government is developing rapidly in Greenland, and increased duties and responsibilities are being given to the Provincial Council.

In 1968, the Provincial Council took over the full responsibility for Greenland's social system. It is now carrying out a plan for social reform that will put Greenland among the most advanced countries in the world. The cost will be borne by Greenland, with a 30 per cent contribution from the Danish Treasury. This reform will not only assist those needing public help and support, but it will aim at inspiring the dynamic development that is so necessary in a country with so few people as 48,000. Investment in social reform will thus be an investment in the country's future.

There is now a system of local government in Greenland that is based on the Danish. Each of the 19 local government areas has its own council, whose members are directly elected for four-year terms.

HOUSING

Housing is the third largest item of government expenditure. There are now 10,200 dwellings in Greenland, of which only 2,500 were built before 1953. The new buildings are crowded, for the housing problem is by no means solved.

In a country where low temperatures, snow, gales, and darkness are major factors, homes must give shelter and security. The actual buildings must be stout, sturdy, and protective. Town developments must provide snug shelter and still allow ready access to land, sunlight and sea. Town planners and architects in

Large-scale building projects like this one in Frederikshaab have been carried out in other Greenland towns in the past few years.

Greenland have tried to give each township an identity of its own by harmonizing various elements of the building style with the special characteristics of the locality.

In Godthaab, for example, they have done this very successfully. This town is situated on a promontory, with mountain ridges running lengthwise. The buildings have been planned to follow this general line, which gives the maximum amount of sunshine for homes and offices. In the sheltered valleys between the ridges, there is rich vegetation. A level plain in the heart of the township, formerly a green swamp, is now built up with homes, schools, institutions, and a town hall.

In summer the grass grows high around this modern home built of field stone and wood, in southern Greenland.

45

This family lives in a modern apartment. More and more housing of this type is being built in Greenland.

MEDICAL FACILITIES

Greenland is divided into 17 medical districts, each with a district medical officer who is also head of the district hospital and a general practitioner. All medical and dental treatment is given free of charge, and the doctors receive fixed salaries.

The greatest problem facing the health authorities formerly was the prevalence of tuberculosis, the most common cause of death. To combat the disease, an intensive scheme for improving the health services was carried out. The Queen Ingrid Tuberculosis Sanitarium was built at Godthaab in 1954, and effective methods for treatment were initiated. Although

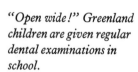

"Open wide!" Greenland children are given regular dental examinations in school.

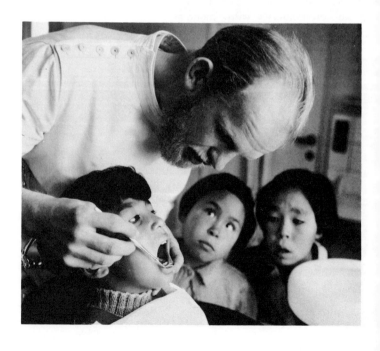

Modern Eskimos wear clothes manufactured in Greenland and are no longer dependent on the seal for home-made clothing.

tuberculosis has not been completely eradicated, there are now practically no deaths in Greenland due to this disease. The Tuberculosis Sanitarium is now a general hospital with 200 beds and with surgical, medical, and TB wards, and a psychiatric ward in the planning stage.

In addition to the Queen Ingrid Hospital, built on the personal initiative of the Danish Queen, there are 17 hospitals strung out along the west coast of Greenland. In 1973, there were 42 doctors, 18 dentists, 129 nurses, 15 certified midwives, and 204 locally trained midwives.

CHANGES IN GREENLAND

The changes that are taking place in Greenland have taken longer than was at first expected, and no one can say when a "normal" existence will come about or what form it will take. But one thing is clear—it is up to the Greenlanders themselves to decide the basis on which their future will rest.

When Greenland's colonial status came to an end and it became an integral part of the Kingdom of Denmark, Greenlanders assumed that this equality of political status meant a speedy development towards equality in other respects. Greenland politics were therefore animated by a desire for equality and the "normalization" of relations between Green-

A Greenland girl wears the bright blouse that, with trousers and high boots, is part of the national costume.

47

These immense radar screens were put up by the United States in Thule, as part of the American early-warning system.

land and the rest of the kingdom, based on the equal political status that had been achieved. As a result, the standard of living has been raised considerably, health and housing standards have been improved, wages have risen, facilities for training have been expanded, and the powers of Greenlandic authorities have been widened.

As the first elected Chairman of the Greenland Provincial Council remarked, "We draw our courage to face the future from our confidence in the continued, unselfish support of our Danish fellow-countrymen and our knowledge of the skill and strength of our Eskimo forefathers in overcoming even the most daunting of natural obstacles. We want to be worthy heirs of a great past. Our destiny is as theirs was: to inhabit the most inhospitable region in the world, facing a constantly threatening sea, with the ice-cap behind us and the North Pole and Arctic Ocean nearest to us."

THULE BASE

When Denmark joined the North Atlantic Treaty Organization, it agreed to maintain some of the World War II military establishments in Greenland. The most important of these today is the base at Thule, which forms part of the United States early-warning system. The base is equipped with immense radar screens with a range of over 3,000 miles. When the Thule base was set up, the local hunting population moved 60 miles farther north and there established a new settlement.

Floating ice in the bay at Christianshaab is no deterrent to the many fishing boats, both large and small.

5. THE ECONOMY

FOR HUNDREDS of years, hunting and trapping provided the Greenlanders with everything they needed. The island was cut off from the rest of the world, and there was no need for it to be otherwise. Those days are now gone. The climate has changed, sending the seals farther north, and air travel has brought the outside world very near.

It has been a slow and difficult process to turn the Greenlander from hunter into fisherman. The hunter was proud of his craft, while fishing was a job for women and children. In the old hunting society, fishing was regarded as an undignified occupation for a man, to be pursued only in case of emergency. The change from a free, independent life to the more routine, humdrum existence of a fisherman was therefore not easy. Hunting, however, has by no means been given up, especially on the east coast.

Even today, an Eskimo would be lost without his kayak, in which he can travel swiftly and with little effort.

HUNTING AND WHALING

In the north and east, about 1,000 families live like their ancestors by catching seals, whales, polar bears, foxes, reindeer, and birds. The hunter still builds his own kayak and makes the tools he needs to survive, while his wife skins the seals and processes the skins. In his kayak, with his own clothes fastened to the covering of the craft, the hunter is all of a piece with his boat. Should he capsize, he can right himself by means of the narrow-bladed double oar.

The all-important harpoon was developed by the Eskimo in the course of 4,000 years. It was originally tipped with reindeer antler or walrus ivory, but these were among the first things to be changed for metal after contact with Europeans. A strong hunter can throw a harpoon about 60 feet.

SEALS AND WALRUSES

Sealing is still the main occupation for many people in north and east Greenland, where seal hunts sometimes last for several days. To protect their eyes from the glare of the snow and ice, hunters use special shades, which are beautifully decorated with bone ornaments.

Whales are still occasionally landed at Godthaab, and fresh whale meat is greatly preferred to the frozen meat in the supermarkets. These boys are feeling the corrugated underside of a whale.

Many modern Greenlanders use a rifle, instead of a harpoon, for securing such animals as seals, whales, polar bears, and the like.

A fleet sets out in kayaks to catch seals, while two children bid them "good hunting."

When the men come back from the hunt the youngsters help haul a seal ashore.

Some 60,000 to 70,000 seals are caught each year. About 80 per cent of the animals belong to the hooded, bearded, and spotted species. The flesh is eaten and some of the skins are used for clothing or for making kayaks. Most of the seal-skins, however, are now sold to the Royal Trading Company for resale at fur auctions in Copenhagen. The walrus, large cousin of the seals, has had to be protected by strict regulations. Today this animal is hunted mainly for its great tusks, which are used for making carved art works.

FOXES AND BEARS

The white Arctic fox is found nearly all over Greenland, where it lives on lemmings, mice, and birds. The blue fox is found principally in cliff areas where nesting sea birds are numerous. The highest-priced skin is that of the polar bear, but hunting this animal is difficult and dangerous. Hunters with their dog sledges can pursue a bear so far out to sea on drift ice as to be driven by changing winds 500 miles across to Canada. One year they may get 50 or 60 bears, the next year only six.

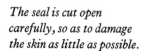

The seal is cut open carefully, so as to damage the skin as little as possible.

When a polar bear can walk no farther on the ice floes, he plunges into the water and tries to swim away from his pursuer.

REINDEER

It is estimated that there are still 12,000 wild reindeer in west Greenland, but about 60 years ago they suddenly disappeared from the east coast. Although the short hunting season falls during the best fishing season, many Greenlanders prefer the excitement of a reindeer hunt to the more profitable fishing. While out hunting, they eat all the reindeer meat they can and dry the rest for use later. At one time the reindeer fur was used for clothing, but now it is used mostly for sledge covers. In 1952, some 300 tame reindeer were brought from Norway, and now there are 5,000 of these animals. The Greenlanders were taught how to tend the new reindeer by Norwegian Lapps. The Lapps, a remarkable group of Arctic no-mads who live on the northern tip of Norway, Sweden and Finland, have long used the reindeer as a domestic animal.

WHALES

For many years the Royal Greenland Trading Company used a large vessel for whaling in west Greenland waters, but today large trawlers, using a harpoon cannon, are more practical. A great many whales of many species are caught in both west and north Greenland waters. The total may be as many as 500 white whales, 125 narwhals, 900 porpoises, 200 lesser rorquals, and 140 pilot whales. The flesh and the inner skin, which has a high vitamin C content, are considered a delicacy by the Greenlanders.

The whale has also been a useful animal to the Eskimo, supplying food, light and heat (from the blubber), as well as many products like oil and whalebone that are sold to other lands.

FISHING

Nearly a third of all Greenlanders now live by fishing. Although they catch 1,200 tons of salmon and 8,400 tons of shrimp a year, both are luxuries in Greenland. The Greenlander still prefers boiled seal, of which he never seems to grow tired.

For a long time, fishing was carried out from small boats or canvas dinghies in the waters of the fjords or along the coast and the catch was either dried or salted. The introduction of trawlers came very slowly. The fishing boats in use now are larger and better equipped, and in the last few years sea-going vessels have been obtained which can operate in all seasons on the rich fishing banks off the west coast of Greenland.

In record time, the Greenland fisherman has made the leap from the kayak, via the sailing craft and small motor boat, to the line vessel (a craft employing lines rather than nets) and trawler. The skippers, however, are still Danes, Norwegians, and Faroese (the people of the Danish-owned Faroe Islands, which lie between Iceland and Norway).

PROBLEMS

Modern methods of fishing require an extensive division of work, as well as large investments of capital. To provide the trained people needed to operate a large trawler, the Greenlanders have had to accustom themselves to fixed working hours and to being organized into trade unions for regulating prices and wages, working hours, and other conditions of employment.

Fishing is a highly competitive business, and for years foreign fishermen were making

Modern trawlers, supplied by the Greenland Trade Department, enable today's fishermen to compete with those of other countries.

fortunes from the great fishing banks off the west coast of Greenland. To meet this competition, the government provided four line vessels, three stern trawlers, 900 motor craft or cutters, and 1,400 rowing vessels with outboard motors. On shore, there are now 60 state-owned and 14 commercial factories for processing fish. In spite of all this help to the Greenlanders, foreign fishermen still make the biggest hauls and the fishing industry operates at a loss.

One reason for the loss is the change of climate, which has brought enormous icebergs and ice-floes along the west coast where fishing takes place, and the water temperature has fallen. As a result of colder water, the stock of cod has declined heavily. In addition, an agreement between Denmark and other fishing nations caused the Danish government to set a limit on the number of salmon that Greenlanders may catch. A third factor is that of world competition. When large shrimp beds were found in Alaska, the discovery had a noticeable effect on Greenland sales.

The fish drying here are not large enough to pack, and will later be fed to the family dogs.

55

The shrimp-packing plant at Christianshaab operates under the most modern and sanitary conditions.

SHRIMP

In 1948, two of the largest shrimp beds in the world were discovered in Disko Bay, and this started an exciting new industry for Greenland. A cannery was erected at Christianshaab and now cutters of 15 to 20 tons from all along the coast are engaged in shrimp fishing. They can supply several factories with freshly caught deep-sea shrimp every day. These canned Greenland shrimp are now exported to 50 countries.

THE FISHING CAPITAL

At Sukkertoppen, fishing is carried out the year round from small motor vessels which operate from 7 to 15 miles from the coast, and the town has become the hub of the fishing industry. A processing plant was set up early in the 1950's and has been expanded since then. Sukkertoppen now has a fish-meal factory, which uses the trimmed waste from the filleting plant, and today most of the town's 2,300 people depend upon fishing for their

Boxes of freshly packed fish are lowered into the hold, ready for shipping.

The salted or frozen fish are packed in barrels (foreground) and sent by large freighters to Europe or America.

living. There are new piers for large ships as well as for the smaller vessels, and also a boatyard and motor depot for repairs.

TYPES OF FISH

The wolf-fish is caught all along the west coast as far north as Upernavik, but is especially plentiful off Sukkertoppen.

The Greenland halibut has become an important export since it can be caught the year round. In summer, halibut are caught in the open waters, but, in winter, fishing for them takes place in the fjords through holes in the ice.

In the old days, the skilled hunters carried a special harpoon in their kayaks and harpooned the salmon when it leapt into the air. Today, most salmon fishing is done by net. Few of the salmon go up Greenland rivers to spawn as they do in other countries. Salmon are quick-frozen and sold to the United States and Denmark. Char are plentiful in rivers and lakes, and are salted in barrels and sold to Sweden.

The seas around Greenland mark the northern limit for cod. Because the cod is very sensitive to variations in temperature, the catch can vary considerably from year to year and in different areas. Greenland cod is exported in salted condition, mostly to Greece, Italy and Spain. When dried and salted, it is sent to Brazil, and plain dried cod (called stockfish) is shipped to Africa.

A modern machine supplies the chipped ice needed in packing fish.

Delicate-looking kayaks bob along with modern trawlers in the ice-clogged waters of a fjord.

Jacobshavn has an excellent port, which is one reason it has grown steadily since it was founded.

These young people are off to the grazing land to move the sheep to fresh pastures. Their sturdy ponies are of the Iceland breed, introduced by the Danes.

SHEEP RAISING

In the extreme south, another occupation is carried on much as it was in the time of Eric the Red. Where the old Viking's sheep and horses used to graze, there are now 150 families who live by sheep farming and growing vegetables. Horses and the old-time Viking ships have been replaced by tractors and motor boats.

Natural conditions for sheep breeding are good in the valleys around Julianehaab, Nonortalik, and Narssaq. In modern times, the first sheep were introduced in 1906. In 1915,

Salmon are often caught by anglers and are considered a great delicacy.

Greenland's few roads are, like the one in the foreground, unpaved.

the government established a sheep station for breeding sheep and training sheep farmers. The sheep have now become the foremost domesticated animals, in place of the sledge dog, which still number about 14,000. There are now some 43,000 sheep in Greenland, which is more, per capita, than in Iceland or the Faroe Islands. If the winter is unusually severe, however, the sheep breeders in Greenland may suffer severe losses.

MINING

The only cryolite mine in the world is found at Ivigtut. The actual mining of this substance, which is important in the production of aluminum, has now ceased, but the cryolite waste, previously neglected, will provide shipments for many years to come. Recent explorations indicate that deposits of other ores including uranium and thorium may be mined profitably.

On a mountain whose name means Black Angel, on the Umanak Fjord, a lead and zinc deposit of possibly 15,000,000 tons is being explored. A deposit of iron ore estimated at 2,000,000,000 tons has been located on the Godthaab Fjord, and a mountain at Narssaq contains at least 200,000 tons of uranium. Molybdenum, used for tempering steel, has been found in eastern Greenland in a deposit amounting to 120,000,000 tons of ore. Just south of Godthaab, a large find of chromium and nickel has been made. Platinum can probably be extracted as a by-product.

Intensive prospecting for oil has also begun. More than a score of the world's leading oil companies want to begin drilling on the continental shelf off the west coast of Greenland in Davis Strait. Experts have predicted that big finds of oil will be made.

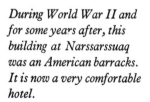

During World War II and for some years after, this building at Narssarssuaq was an American barracks. It is now a very comfortable hotel.

The Hotel Hvide Falk (White Falcon) in Jacobshavn, the first hotel in Greenland built especially for tourists, was opened in 1971.

OTHER ACTIVITIES

Because of the intensive technological development, more and more people have turned from the traditional occupations to trades, crafts, and services. Greenland now has 300 craft and contracting firms and 160 commercial traders, in addition to government establishments and co-operatives. Unfortunately for the Greenlanders, however, most private enterprise is still in Danish hands.

Tourism has been steadily growing since Greenland was opened to the outside world. Previously, anyone who wished to visit the big island had to get special permission from the Danish government. That is no longer necessary. Instead, there are a number of well-planned tours to various parts of Greenland that may be taken from Denmark, England, or Iceland. There are no direct flights from the United States. Comfortable hotels are located in

Of the 26 double rooms in the White Falcon Hotel, Jacobshavn, 20 have private bathrooms.

Enterprising Greenland children offer necklaces and furs for sale to the tourists.

several communities, and all-day excursions to various points of interest. There are now about 2,000 tourists a year who visit this amazing land. It is so completely different from any other part of the world that its appeal for travellers is bound to grow.

It need hardly be pointed out that the only time to visit Greenland as a tourist is in the summer. Apart from the scenic and historic points of interest, there are many modern shops in Greenland, where visitors may buy such popular Danish goods as glassware, furniture and porcelain.

A "piggy-back" ride is always fun, and these Greenland children are strong enough to give rides to younger brothers and sisters who are nearly as large as they are.

Tourists who want a new thrill can ride on a dog sledge. Though once a necessity to the Greenlander, these dog sledges and their teams are seldom used now except to entertain visitors.

An attractive fountain adorns the market place of Julianehaab, one of the oldest settlements in Greenland.

INDEX